Speakin'

The

Gospel

Truth

Lady V

Lord I Sacrifice

Lord, today I sacrifice my life to you

Not because I have to

But because I choose to

I know I may have strayed away

And lost my way

But your love for me always remains the same

And today, here I stand

Surrendering it all

Giving my life back to you

Here I am on bended knees

Asking for you to please forgive me

Please, show me how to get back to you

Today, I'm reaching out my hand

Trying to grab a hold of you

Asking for your forgiveness

Letting you know

I'm sacrificing it all for you

I no longer want to walk on this burning fence

Of chaos...grief...and foolishness

When it's so much cooler where you are

Where the streets are paved in gold

Thanks for giving me a better way

Showering me with brighter days

Thanks for your constant love

This is the day I've been dreaming of

So today I come before you

Sacrificing my all to you

Just so I can be close to you

Even when I'm not worthy of your love

Thanks for washing away all my sins

Making me whole and new again

Lord, I will sacrifice for you on a daily basis

Letting your light shine through me

As your people see you live inside of me

Each and every day

Guiding every step I take

Orchestrating every breath I make

Giving you a crazy praise

Making a joyful noise

Today, I sacrifice my life for you

Rededicating my life back to you

Praising you like no other

Placing my faith over my fear

Lord...today, this is my sacrifice

I'm ready to come home

Giving my life back to you

Walking and living my purpose

Doing all the things you ask of me

Today, I sacrifice my life

And give it back to you

Running Away

I'm running…

Running in circles

Circles of my mind

Trying to figure out where I stand

Where I belong

When nothing makes sense

And everything I thought I knew

Doesn't exist

How long has my heart been accepting this emptiness?

Am I just an illusion of what used to be?

A shell made up of darkness

A glass half empty

That once was full

Screaming…

Because they can't see me

Simply can't see the pain they're causing me

Is it because they've forgotten about me?

Well now you know...

Why I keep running away

Why stay where you're not loved... not welcomed...

And nobody recognizes you

But somewhere over the rainbow

Is a celebration just for me

Where many mansions are built

Receiving all the roses I am due

I can't keep running from this pain I've endured all my life

When there's something better

Waiting on the other side

Just for lil ole me

Then I won't be running from a lifetime full of pain

But running to a lifetime full of gain

And I'm not talking about laundry detergent

But a glow up

Letting them know I've showed up

And nothing can kill...steal...or destroy the God in me

Instead of running

I will walk away from toxicity

And run towards God's unconditional love

The one thing that never changes

Even when man is wearing sheep's clothing

And their mask is two-faced

In God's basic instructions

He said no weapon formed against me shall prosper

He never said they wouldn't form

Now why would he lie?

When he stands on all his promises

Always staying true to his word

So instead of running away

Hiding from what God intended for me

Because you're embarrassed of my true identity

But don't fret

I will continue running towards the finish line

Where God is standing

Waiting for me with open arms

And his unconditional love

He's the only one I will be running too

I Am Not A Loser

I am not a loser

Can you hear me loud and clear?

Or is my yell a simple whisper?

Making you struggle to hear what I'm saying to you

You see...

For some reason you can't seem to hear me

It's as if I've been put on mute

Am I being silenced?

Silenced from speaking the truth

Or silenced from being the person you think I don't
deserve to be

Well...you forgot one thing...

God made me great

You can never count me out

But somehow you keep saying...

I'm a loser

Is it because my hair is not curly enough for you?

Maybe…it's because my eyes are not blue enough for you

No…No…No…

Wait one minute

It must be because my tone ain't proper enough for you

I'm not really sure what it is

But I know one thing for sure

I must get you straight

Please don't take this as disrespectful

Because the words I say

Aren't made up of fantasy lies

I coming with the rolling thunder

Slicing and dicing the negativity

You placed upon my name

You already know my tongue is a lethal weapon

More lethal than any sword

And my truth is hot like fire

So brutal…

Giving you third degree burns

But like mama used to say...

If you can't stand the heat

Get out the kitchen

This heat you don't want

When God fights all of my battles

And can't be beat

Apparently you feel on top of the world

Choosing to ruffle these old rugged feathers

Making me go to the mainline

Telling God what I really want

So I don't snap on you

Coming out of my character

Making me do something I may later regret

So I have to call upon him

Because he's not through working on my yet

And I still have some of that gangsta in me left

You see...

My hair may not be curly and blonde

It's nappy...kinky...and loc'd up

Representing my natural beauty

With no added preservatives

No fakeness...making you believe you're something you're not

Sitting on top of the world

Looking down on others

When God says judge thee not

So no...

I don't have blue eyes

And that's okay

You may think you're hiding your skeletons

But I'm sorry to say

We can see straight through you

I can go on and on

But then that would be annihilating you

And I'm about uplifting God's people

Not tearing them down

When God clearly tells me to uplift his people

And build one another up

So that we shall walk and not faint

So no...I am not a loser

No matter how you may feel

You see...

God made something special when he made me

Breaking the mold

Making no mistakes

Making me real

And never fake

I am not a loser

I'm God's anointed one

His chosen one

So be careful when you put your mouth on me

Thinking I'm not worthy of God's unconditional love

But I've got news for you

God loves me regardless of what you may think

No matter what man says

You no longer have control over me

When I serve a God greater than thee

Who holds all the power in his hands

And you can't crucify me

No matter how much you may try

I wear the whole armor of God

You can't touch me

When God's hedge of protection is all around me

So...call me what you want

Say what you want about me

But...I am not a loser

God lives and rests inside me

Going everywhere I go

Making a boss out of me

As I spread my wings

And fly like an eagle

Making waves in the sky

Creating a beautiful masterpiece

Speakin' nothing...

But that Gospel Truth

God's Masterpiece

Beauty is in the eye of the beholder

But what happens when the world can see you through
God's eyes

One of his most precious masterpieces

Glowing for all to see

Not your outer beauty

But the beauty from within

You see...

Each day you walk with him

The layers begin to fall off

As you blossom into something so beautiful

It's delicate like a flower

Fragile to the touch

Spreading your wings

Showing all your beautiful colors

Releasing all those evil thoughts

Where depression

Sadness

And suicide lies

Because people have destroyed the very essence of you

Destroying God's greatest masterpiece

Making you feel unworthy

Of God's precious love

Exposing you to the devils truth

But God is saying to you

No weapon can prosper against you

He never said it wouldn't form

It's time for you to wake up

Open your eyes

Look in the mirror

You will see God's greatest masterpiece

Standing in front of you

Waiting for you to see

God's greatest masterpiece

God made no mistakes

When he created you

He's just been waiting for you

To come back his way

Knowing where your peace and comfort lies

So here you stand

At the golden gates

Ready to be made new

Ready to strip down

Be cleansed of all your sins

But the one thing you forgot

God paid the ultimate price

So that you can be brand new

No charges held against you

Because you are one of God's greatest masterpieces

Continue to spread your wings

The world is waiting for you

Ready to see the God in you

Live your purpose abundantly

Let the light shine bright inside of you

Spread the gospel truth

Even though it may hurt just a little bit

God will protect you

Letting no danger come upon you

When you are

God's masterpiece

Here I Stand

Here I stand

Asking God why

Not why he took me through all the lessons

But why he chose me

To do his business

When I was so lost and confused

Not knowing which way to turn

But then I heard him say

Because I knew you would be so bold

Giving me all the praise

Then I got on my hands and knees

As I bowed to thee

He said raise my child

I have an assignment for you

So here I stand

Trying to figure out

Which way to run

Where to hide

How do I jump off this ride?

When life was so easy

Doing what I want to do

Doing it my way

But now I've been called

To go somewhere I've never been

Wondering if I'm going to mess things up

How can he trust me so much?

When I barely trust myself

And that small voice is saying...

Girl...you bet not dare

Nobody will listen to you

God won't protect you

Ain't no blessing for you

You can't do that

But here I stand

Ready to take on this new task

Believing that God will carry me through

Casting out those little voices trying to come through

Telling me that God doesn't want me

When he chose me personally

Here I stand

Standing on the battlefield boldly

With the full armor

Doing what I was called to do

Happy Birthday Jesus

Happy Birthday Jesus

Today we celebrate you

Today is your special day

And we give you a crazy praise

For on this day

A star was born

Born in a manger

To a virgin who never complained

But can you imagine her pain?

Delivering a son

With no drugs or comfort

But yet he was so precious

And became a friend of mine

Walking on water to save my soul

Healing the blind so that I can see

Feeding a multitude so I can eat

Now who would do all those things for me?

No one but the king

And his name is King Jesus

Coming from up above

Dying on the cross for me

Forgiving me for all my sins

Cleansing me white as snow

Wiping my slate clean

Charging me nothing

Thank you God for sending your son

The special one

If he does nothing else

He's done enough

Thanks for giving us the best gift

I will never forget

Jesus is the reason for the season

And today we celebrate him

Happy Birthday Jesus

Thanks for all you've done

Today we celebrate you

Magnifying your holy name

God's precious son

Who Do You Trust

Who do you trust?

Is it the government?

The one who continues to make broken promises

As the economy is going up and people are steady dying

Because all they want is a quick buck

Who do you trust?

Is it the neighbor?

The one who keeps stealing your mail

Letting his dog poop in your yard

Who do you trust?

Is it your boss?

The one who refuses to give you a raise for all your hard
work

Never taking notice what you bring to the table

Who do you trust?

Is it your mate?

The one who says they love you

But giving their attention to something or someone else

Never making you a priority

Keeping you in the dark

Spending all your money up

Who do you trust?

Is it the church?

The one who makes you tithe every month

Still working on the building fund

Never giving back

Pastor driving a brand new Cadillac

Who do you trust?

It's something to think about

We keep putting our trust in the wrong things

Thinking that people will love us unconditionally

Thinking that people will see the beauty in us

But somehow...

All we feel is used up

Now ask yourself...

Who do you trust?

I trust in a higher power

The one who carries me through

The one who gave his life for me

The one who died on the cross for me

The one who never leaves nor forsakes me

The one who forgives me of all my sins

The one who never judges

The one who gives me warning before the storm

I could go on and on

But I think you get the point

But if you don't

You've already messed up

Because God is the only one I will put my trust

When I gave my life to him

I finally found peace

Beginning to love my inner man

Seeing how beautiful he created me

Needing no validation

When he made me perfect in his own image

It doesn't matter how they see me

When God loves me unconditionally

Even when I wasn't deserving of his love

He still forgave me of all my sins

And that's why God is the only one I trust

He's never told anyone my darkest secrets

Never held it against me

Never told a lie to me or on me

He's more than just someone I know

He's my best friend

We talk every day

Laughing with me

Collecting each tear

Planting my beautiful garden

No matter how ugly it may look

And you ask...

Who do I trust?

I trust the one who sacrificed his life for me

So that I could have eternal life

And I plan on living my best life

But not trusting man

Who will turn on me in a blink of an eye

Charging me with a crime I didn't commit

But like they say...

I'm guilty until proven innocent

And that's why I can't trust man

I'd rather take my chances with the man up above

Because I'm always innocent

No matter the charge

When he forgave me of all my sins

I will continue walking with him

Putting all my trust

He never lost a battle

And will never lose a war

All I can say is...

You better choose wisely

And ask yourself

Who do you trust?

Navigation Street

Can someone tell me how I get to the kingdom?

They say I can find it this way

On Navigation Street

Where it's ok to come as you are

A place for the lost

Would you say this is true?

Suddenly a soft voice says...

Keep straight

But don't fall off the beaten path

So on my journey I continue on my way

Looking for the one who can save my life

Forgiving me of all my sins

Now where would I be if he hadn't given his life for me?

So that I can live life abundantly

I guess one thing's for sure

I wouldn't be on Navigation Street

Trying to find my way to the kingdom

The one they call heaven

Someone told me I could find it this way

But don't go off the beaten path

But it looks like I've gotten lost

The enemy has tricked me

Made me think that I was still on Navigation Street

But in reality

I'm on Hells Paradise

Please...Please...Please

Can someone help me get out of this nightmare?

The nightmare where sadness...drama...and toxic
situations exist

I don't want to be here anymore

But I'm having trouble finding my way back

And people I thought loved me

Keep turning their back

Will someone help me turn back the hand of time?

Rescue me out of this forest of sorrow and deceit

Who can I turn to?

How do I get back to Navigation Street?

Then a man in a Cadillac

Pulled up and rescued me

All because God told me to follow his voice

Now I could've listened to the one in my head

Telling me to keep straight ahead

Down the path I know is no good

But then he held out his hand for me

Telling me to go the other way

Scared at first

I allowed him to lead the way

Leading me back to Navigation Street

Where the Kingdom exist

Where happiness...love...and joy reside

This thing called life may not be easy

And there will be some turns along the way

But don't let the devil have his way

Or you will find yourself in Hells Paradise

When Navigation Street is where you want to be

The road may be a little bumpy

And the path may not be straight

But always remember...

Let God have his way

He will never lead you astray or give up on you

He's there to forever stay

Making sure you have brighter days

But you have to trust

Stand on your faith

Allow God to lead you down the beaten path...

Of Navigation Street

Speak To Me

Speak to me

Speak to me Lord

Can I hear a word from you?

A word to fill my soul

A word to fill this void

Make me feel whole again

Please Lord

Make me feel brand new

Lord, won't you speak to me?

I need you

Walk through my home

Guide me

Direct me

Show me a better way to go

So much is going on

I need someone I can hold on to

So I lift my hands to thee

Please Lord

Won't you speak to me?

I need to hear a word from you

So come inside the room

I need my daily medicine

I come to give you the highest praise

Because you are my daily bread

I need you each and every day

As I go on about my way

So speak Lord

Please speak to me

Please give me a word to tell your broken children

The one who's looking for your love

But lost in the sauce

The mother struggling to take care of her kids

Who needs to know that you're her provider

Speak Lord

Please speak to me

Give me the words to say

So I can tell it on the mountain top

How good you've been to me

No it' not bragging or boasting

I just gotta share your Goppy love

The one you give me on a daily basis

I want the whole world to know

How good your love is

So speak Lord

Speak to them and me

We need to hear a word from you

Sunshine

Today I can see the sun through the rain

Even on it's cloudiest day

I know you're trying to understand

How can such a thing happen when it's so hard to see past the pain?

Yes...that's how I use to feel

Until I start building a personal relationship with God

Who would've known?

He would heal my broken heart

Repairing all my battle wounds

Putting me back together again

Allowing me to see

The sunshine through the rain

I'm so thankful

For all my brighter days

The one I thought passed me by

Making me seem worthless

When I'm not

Because God created me in his own image

And that's how I can see the sunshine

The one that brightens my day

The one that shines through the rain

All Aboard

All aboard...

Do you have your ticket to ride this train?

This train is going one way

Never to return

Are you sure...this the train you want to get on?

This train won't be going downtown

Or making any sudden stops

This train is on a mission

To do God's business

No holding up traffic

Understanding the assignment

Knowing there's work to do

Before we get to the kingdom of heaven

Where our father is standing

Waiting for us to surrender our lives to thee

So what are we waiting for?

When it's time to get on board

On the train that will save your soul

Making you whole

Giving you life again

Regaining everything that was taken from you

Isn't that worth the sacrifice?

Getting on board

Ready to take a chance

Heading to a better place

Regaining your strength and your peace

Ain't no better place

When you bet on the Lord our savior

He will set you free

From your evil ways

But first you gotta get on board

This train is about to pull out

So don't be alarmed when you hear the horn

And the conductor shouting

All Aboard

This is your last chance

To get with the program

Doing what's best for you

It's time to ride

So will you be on board this train ride?

The choice is up to you

Say No More

Say no more

The devil is listening to you

Hearing every negative thing you say

Laughing

Taking over your life

But it's time to change that around

When God is waiting for you

Ready to give you a brighter life

Allowing you to live life abundantly

But say no more

Maybe you should hum

Allowing God to hear your cry

But say no more

God heard your hum

Understanding every word

Catching every tear

Listening to your inner thoughts

Ready to caress your heart

But you gotta let him in

Know that he's real

And waiting to take your hand

Giving you the plan

He has for your life

But say no more

Your negativity is stopping you

It's time to change that around

Let God take control

And have his way

Make It Go Viral

Let's make it go viral

I'm not talking about that new video

The one they blowing weed smoke

Talking trash

Being disrespectful

Dancing

Or making you laugh

I'm talking about making God's word go viral

It's funny how when you start talking about God

The room goes silent

No one wants to hear about that

But he's the only one who can save you

The one who can give you eternal life

The one who can mend that broken heart

But still...

Nothing

No one wants to make his truth go viral

I guess it's not funny enough

But why?

God has a sense of humor

He laughs at us every day

Then asks his father to forgive us

For we know not what we do

Yet...keep making the same foolish mistakes

Why can't we make his word go viral?

Why can't we make his name go viral?

When he's the one to give his only forgotten son

To die on the cross for us

Is that not worth going viral?

I guess you thought you can do all of this by yourself?

When he's the true reason for the seasons

He's the reason you're breathing

He's the reason you're able to live your best life

Isn't that enough to go viral?

Well I can only speak for myself

And you will be able to see his holy name

Up and down my timeline

No matter what

God will always know

That I thought he was enough

To make him go viral

There's A Leak In This Old Building

There's a leak in this old building and I'm ready to move

I've patched the holes up so many times

But the water is still coming through

The water is rising quickly

I feel like I'm drowning

But I'm holding on

I know a man greater than thee

Who will come to save me

The one who walked on water

The one who made a blind man see

The one who told Martha not to moan

That's who I'm putting all my trust in

To come save me

From this old leaking building

Thanks for throwing me a raft

While preparing a better home for me

I'm holding on

No matter what things may look like

I'm holding on

Even when I think I'm drowning

And can't take no more

I'm holding on

The enemy's plan can't stop me

From waiting on God's unchanging hand

I'm holding on

Because I know he has a better plan for my life

Preparing me a new home in this life

Right here on earth

So I'm holding on

Until I am free to move on

Into my new home

Reaping all the rewards

He promised to give me

For holding on

Now I'm moving on

To my brand new place

Leaving this old leaking building

To be condemned

Leaving it behind me

But not forgetting where I come from

Where I had to stand on my faith

And trust that God will bring me through

But he did everything he said he would do

And now I'm moving on

To a better place

Where I belong

No more patch up jobs

When God fixed every leak

Just like he said he would

If I believe

Tell It Like It Is

Tell it like it is

It's time to stop living a lie

Because it's no better than the truth

And a lie will last for a lifetime

When the truth will set you free

And only hurt for a moment

Tell it like it is

Why would you want to continue to live in misery?

When God said you can live life abundantly

It's time to tell it like it is

I'm not trying to bring you any bad news

But I gotta tell it like it is

When you're allowing media to poison you anyways

Bringing you fake news

Destroying your beliefs

Thinking that the government has your best interest at heart

When you're a pawn

In their corrupted justice system

Thinking you're free

When you're really awarded to the state

A slave

Making you think it's about race

When it's about color

Just not black or white

But green

Greed and Envy

It's time to tell it like it is

So why do we keep fighting against one another?

Creating meaningless wars

When it's easier to join together

But God said things would be this way

But it's up to us to make a change

Destroy the enemy's plans

Make this world a better place

For us to happy in

Celebrating My Blackness

Today and every day I celebrate my blackness

I am not black only twenty eight days out of the year

I am black three sixty five

Every day I celebrate my blackness

The blackness that some hate

The blackness that some don't understand

The blackness that some discriminate against

The blackness that some want to be just like

My melanin skin represents the beauty I am

The beauty I've come from

The one so many fought for

So we can have equal rights

But fifty years later we're still being hunted and shot down
like dogs

Wild animals from a zoo

But somehow even the animals are treated better than blacks

The ones they call African Americans

But somehow we're still not free

When there was a bill passed in 1964

Why are we, still frighten for our lives?

When so many marched and lost their lives so that we can be free?

But God sacrificed the most

So that we can live life abundantly

But yet they still hide behind the bible

And sheets...wolf's clothing

But they can never silent us from celebrating our blackness

Our melanin skin

The one just like Jesus

A darker hue with woolly hair

Revelation 1:14

Today we're speaking the Gospel truth

Making it known

That God is a God who can not and will not lie

His basic instructions tells us everything we need

So today I celebrate my blackness

I'm black and I'm proud

Thank you Malcolm X and Martin Luther King Jr.

For being men of God

But standing on the battlefield for our rights

Although they may not have been on the same course

Your intentions were the same

Thank you Rosa Parks for giving up your seat

I know you were tired and warn out from a long day of work

But you refused to move

And now I can sit anywhere I choose

Thank you Harriet Tubman for leading the slaves to victory

Giving them a new life of freedom

To choose what they want to be

Thank you Madam C.J. Walker for having a plan

Refusing to back down

Becoming the first millionaire hair dresser

Giving black girls the confidence to know that we're
beautiful

No matter of our hair texture

Kinky, nappy, or straight

You made sure we were laid, dyed, and pressed to the side

We will never forget all the things y'all have done

Today and every day

I will celebrate my blackness

My black is beautiful

Shining for the whole world to see

Say What You Like

Say what you like about me

They talked about Jesus Christ

Yet, he still died for you and me

And you still crucified him

So what would make me any better?

When you could harm our Lord and Savior

The one who loved you so

So say what you like about me

Because my journey you will never understand

And my walk will never by your walk

So say what you like

I can only do me

And you can only do you

But remember

The same judgment you place upon me

Will be the same judgment placed upon you

I don't hate you my brother

I don't despise you my sister

In fact...

I pray for you

And ask my father to forgive you

For you know not what you do

To his precious child

And that's okay

Because he forgave you for all your sins

And I will too

You don't have to see the God in me

I will continue to pray

For God to walk inside you

So one day

People will see how God has changed you

So say what you like

You could never change God' plan

He has upon my life

The End of Defeat

You think you may have lost the battle

But God has won the war

You think you have been defeated

But really you've found your strength

In God you may have peace

In the world you will have tribulation

But trust that God has overcome the world

And no weapon formed against you shall prosper

When you can do all things through Christ

Which strengthens you

So how can you be defeated?

When God is standing by your side

Carrying you through

Hold your head up high

Where your help cometh from

And know that God

Will never leave you

Nor forsake you

He will be there

Through the good and bad

All you have to do is lean on him

Casting all your understanding upon him

Watch...

Trust...

Believe...

You are at the end of your defeat

When God is carrying you through

Stand Up...Get Your Praise On

Stand up...get your praise on

What are you waiting for?

Today is the day

To make a joyful noise

Singing the highest praise to our father

Rejoicing and lifting him up

Because he sprinkled you

Waking you up

Giving you life

To enjoy this beautiful...glorious day

So wake up...stand up...

Get your praise on

It's time to get moving

Blessings falling upon you

Doing all the things you love to do

Because our Lord and Savior gave you another day

So rejoice

It's time to be glad in it

Stand up...get your praise on

Hallelujah...Hallelujah

Our Father

Deserves the highest praise

It's time for a crazy praise

So stand up...and get your praise on

John 3:16

For God so loved the world

Wait...you mean God loved all of us?

No matter what religion we are

Yep...So much

That he gave his only begotten son

Wait...you mean the only son he had?

Yep...now who would do that?

Not me or anyone I know

Now why would someone want to sacrifice their own son?

So who so ever believes in him shall not perish but have everlasting life

Now that's something there

You mean all I have to do is believe and live forever?

Yep...now ain't our God good?

So amazing that he loves the whole world and it doesn't matter what color or creed we are

It doesn't matter what religion we are

It doesn't matter what our ethnicity or gender is

God sacrificed his only son for you and me

Now that's love

Something we should show to each other each and every day

God is love

And I love you too

Joy Comes In the Morning

The storm may be brewing

But joy comes in the morning

You may not have all you need

But joy comes in the morning

You may not have all you want

But joy comes in the morning

So why are you holding on to the things of this world?

When God's precious love will give you the peace you
need

And joy comes in the morning

It's okay to fall on your knees

Give it to our Lord up above

And watch as your blessings come down

Because joy comes in the morning

Hold your head up high

Lift your hands to the sky

Know that God heard your prayers

And you will be blessed

For joy comes in the morning

Man In the Mirror

Staring myself down

Looking and trying to figure out my next move

Asking God

What am I to do?

Then that still voice says to me

Look at the man in the mirror

What do you think your next move should be?

I stare at the person looking back at me

Not recognizing who she is

Who in the world have I become

Embarrassed and ashamed of the person looking back at
me

I know God is not pleased with me

But I can't stop doing me

I am too far deep

Too far gone

To stop and let God have his way

But God's plans was not my plans

And I couldn't stop what he had for me

Stopping me in my tracks

Making me plead for my life

Refusing to save me

Making me save myself with his basic instructions

You know...

The ones I refuse to follow

Dragging me like a motorcycle crashing into the pavement

Making me take a deeper look at my life

Observing where I really want to be

And this side of the fence got me changing my mind

Ready to go back to the other side of the street

Begging God to forgive me

For I have sinned

I'm ready to do the right things

Live the right way

Begging for my life

Please God, forgive me

Help me out of this dark tunnel

Giving me my basic instructions one more time

I was able to find my way to the son

Giving my life back to where my help comes from

Not taking for granted his precious love

Now when I stare at the man in the mirror looking back at me

I'm proud of how far she's come

Overcoming obstacles that tried to stop her

To living her life abundantly

Not my way

But God's way

At some point we have to evaluate and examine the man in the mirror

Asking it...

Am I living?

Or just existing

Today I choose to live my life in peace and harmony

Thanking God for every day of my life

Especially when tomorrow is not promised to me

I must live for today

AS if it was my last

Looking at the man in the mirror

Was like looking at a blast from the past

All I know is...

I never want to go there again

It's not worth risking my life

When I live for my Lord and Savior now

He makes my bad days turn good

My cloudy days turn bright

And fill my life with peace

I will not look back

When God has saved me from my past

Making me better than I was yesterday

I will forever hold his hand

So when I look at the man in the mirror

I can recognize her

And know God is proud of who I am

Lord I Look to You

Lord I look to you

There's no man I can trust quite like you

You build me up

When I am torn down

You place my feet on solid ground

Man could never replace you

Man can't love me like you do

Thanks for giving me your goppy love

There's no other love like yours

So kind

So gentle and pure

Thanks for letting your love rain down upon me

No one can do me like you

So Lord I look to you in all I do

I will never put anyone above you

You are the head and not the tail of my life

I can't make it without you

I will make every sacrifice

Just for you to be in my life

This may sound like a love letter

And in a way it kinda is

But this goes to my Father up above

The ruler of my life

The one I will continue to lean upon

Lord, I will look to you

For the rest of my life

You Don't Have to Like Me

You don't have to like me

But in God's basic instructions

He commands you to love me

In spite of my flaws and evil ways

God commands us to love all of his children

Even the ones who trespass against us

So you don't have to like me

But God commands for you to love me

I may not be perfect

And my truth may be brutal

But I only speak the words that I hear

And as we know it...

The truth hurt sometimes

But sometimes we have to say it

So you don't have to like me

But the truth will set you free

You don't have to like the way I look, or dress

You don't have to like the way I speak

Maybe it's a little too aggressive for you

My pitch or tone may not have come out right

But I'm a sinner saved by grace

Don't think that because I praise God

I don't sin every day

I'm not different than you

Sometimes I just sing a different tune

And that's okay

Because we praise the same

So no...

You don't have to like me

And I don't have to like you

But according to God's basic instructions

The only one I follow

He commands us to love one another

Each and every day

So my brother and sister

I may not like you

And you may not like me

But every day, I will continue to love and pray for you

Even when deep in my heart

I know how we truly feel

And trust...

The feeling is mutual

Toxic Waste

OMG...what is this?

It's sticky and it stinks

Some call it nasty

Some call it toxic waste

Something that always trying to get in your way

Keeping you lost and displaced

Always in mix company

Of confusion and catastrophe

I'm trying to understand

Why does it keep finding me?

Does it know me by name?

Maybe it has my address...

But is that even possible?

When I've moved since then

But somehow

It keeps knocking at my front door

Trying to come in

Making itself at home

Destroying Gods perfect place

Well, today I saw it walking down the street

And I knew it was looking for me

But it couldn't find me

Because I was layered up

I had on my full protection

Throwing it off my scent

Instead it went next door

Calling me by name

I heard the neighbors say...

She doesn't live on this street

Looking around

Confused and in a daze

It couldn't believe that it couldn't find me

So it continued down the street

Going from house to house

Calling out my name

Wondering why its call isn't being answered

Until it got to the end of the road

And realized it's on Jesus Street

The one who protects me

The one who sacrificed his life for me

No toxic waste will ever enter into my life again

No matter who or what it may be

I have no room for any negative energy

You can take that somewhere else

Toxic waste isn't welcomed anymore

Now move around

Find someone else to disturb

Because God's Saints

Got our foot on your neck

We will not be defeated or disturbed

This block ain't to be touched

This is God's sacred land

And he holds all the power in his hands

Use me Lord, I'll go

So many years I fought you

Wanting to do it my way

Thinking that I had no other alternative

When the street life was looking so glamorous

Now I could paint a perfect picture

Because I was in it to win it

Nothing could stop the life I was choosing to live

But in reality

As things were good

So were they bad

But through the pain

You were telling me to come home

As I look back

I ask myself

Why was I so stubborn?

Why was I so adamant about living that life?

When the pain outweighed the good

But I got the lesson

Even if it took me a little bit longer

I understand now, Father

Thank you for being a God of second chances

Forgiving me

When I couldn't forgive myself

I was so lost and afraid

Yet you found and still wanted to save me

Finding me still worthy of your love

Now all I can say is…

Lord use me

I will spread your word

Telling the world how great you are

How you saved a wretch like me

Stripping me from my comfort zone

Making a better woman out of me

Someone I didn't know I could be

Lord use me

I will spread your love all across the land

Making them see

The love of you shining within me

So Lord keep using me

I will prevail

I will go wherever you need me to be

So Shall I Wait

The hardest thing to do

Is except the truth

No matter how much you brace yourself

It's still a hard pill to swallow

But once you do

It's not for you to weep in sorrow

So shall I wait on you Lord

Although my heart feels empty

It's full of you

That's why I'm not feeling sad or blue

Sometimes the loneliness seeps in

Then I began to remember

That you are close to me

When your word says...

You will never leave

Or forsake me

So I guess I knew this day was coming

That the one I love

Doesn't love me

It's funny how it falls that way

But so shall I wait on you Lord

To fill that empty void

That starts to fill this empty room

Oh Lord what shall I do?

When I've learned to love me

And done all you've asked

Am I not worthy of love?

How do I fill this void?

So shall I wait on you Lord

I'm waiting to hear an answer from you

I'm waiting to hear a word from you

What shall I do?

So I sit patiently and wait

Waiting to hear the voice of the Lord

And there it was sitting right in front of me

While I'm looking somewhere else

It was sitting patiently

Waiting for me

Loving me right

Listening to what I have to say

Being my best friend

Everything I am looking for

But yet I couldn't see it that way

When God had set it up that way

Why do we continue hurting ourselves?

When sometimes the answer is simple

Waiting for the hurt to come

From a love that never loved us

When God's love is all around us

But we call them just a friend

When God is a friend indeed to me

Stopping looking at the one you can't have

When the one God wants you to have

Is starring you right in the face

Ready to give you all the love your heart desires

And so much more

Why continue to be an afterthought

When God loves you much more

So shall I wait on you Lord

Broken

I'm broken

But I'm being set free

Set free of the mindset

The enemy thought it had on me

I'm broken

But I'm being set free

Set free of the hurt and pain

My actions and past have caused me

I'm broken

But I'm being set free

Set free of the evil thoughts

Satan tried to make me believe

I'm broken

But I'm being set free

Set free of the negative energy

Being placed around me

I'm walking away

I can hear the chains falling up off of me

I am no longer who or what I used to be

I'm being set free

Of whatever you thought about me

I no longer carry that title

When all I follow is the B.I.B.L.E.

You know...

The Basic Instructions Before Leaving Earth

The one who knows how to comfort me

Comfort me through my brokenness

Comfort me through the hurt and pain

Putting me back together again

When all man has ever left me with

Is heartache and shame

Always using my wrongs

To crucify me

Beating me down

When they really have nothing to gain

I may be broken

But I can hold my head up high

Because God forgave me

When he laid down his life

For you and I

Paying the ultimate price

Saying...

No Charge

Wiping all my debts away

So I will rejoice through my brokenness

For he's healed me twice

Giving me a new life

To try all over again

Stop..Look..Listen

Stop...Look...Listen

God is trying to talk to you

Why do you keep going that way?

When God's plan is the only way

Do you not believe or trust in him?

When he's trying to set you free

Setting you free of your evil ways

Setting you free of the thoughts consuming you

Stop...Look...Listen

God is trying to lead the way

But yet you want to keep going astray

Do you not believe that the path of righteousness

Is the better way

Stop...Look...Listen

Your boat is about to crash

Crash into the ocean of darkness

Never to be seen again

You see my story could've ended this way

But he landed me in the forest

Far far away

I could hear the traffic

But couldn't find my way

I had to

Stop...Look...Listen

To the voice of God

So I could find my way to him

I remember that sweet beautiful day

When there he await

Waiting on me to come to the side

Where peace...joy...and happiness lye

I just had to get out of my own way

And make better choices

So I tell you my friend

Don't be like me

Get like me

And let the Lord have his way

You will be in a better place

Only if you

Stop...Look...and Listen

Whose Children Are You?

The old Lady across the street would yell at us

Whose children are you?

And we would yell the same thing every day

She asked that same question every day

Until the day she died

And although we wondered why

We never questioned her

Well the other day

I heard someone say

Whose children are you?

I froze

Thinking...

Could it be her?

Has she risen from the dead?

Then I heard it again

Whose children are you?

I wanted to yell out

But my vocals was frozen

Like wings on a fly

During a winter storm

Standing still

Waiting to hear the voice again

Oh how it suddenly changed

Asking me again

Whose children are you?

As I wanted to scream out

Like I was a child

I remembered everything that was taught to me

So I answered in a stern but steady voice

I am the child of the Lord

The one who saved me

The one who died on the cross for me

The one who was crucified for me

The one who loves me unconditionally

Then I heard

Go on my child

You have answered correctly

You know who you belong to

So when someone asks you

Whose children are you?

Remember to whom you belong

God is your mother and father

God is our Lord and Savior

God is our rescuer

God is the only parent I know

Thank you Lord

For choosing me

When everyone else

Doubted me

Thank you Lord

For choosing me

When everyone else

Could never see the good in me

Thank you Lord for choosing me

When everyone else

Had already casted me out

So no...man don't have to see me

When God has already chosen me

And that's to whom I belong

Let Your Truth Set You Free

So you have something to say?

Well, let your truth set you free

But don't worry to how I will react

No...I'm not going to go crazy

Blessing you out

Acting like I don't know who created me

So please...

Let your truth set you free

Just know...

Your words can't hurt me anymore

When I've always known how you felt about me

I just had to learn to accept

Your constant attacks

Shooting off like a missile

Thinking I'm your enemy

When I'm really your daughter

But don't worry about me

I know how to get out of your way

So I don't blow up

Coming out of my character

Making me become something I don't want to be

Letting this lion

Out of it's cage

When it's not tamed

And don't know how to behave

That's why I stay close to the father

The one who keeps forgiving me

For falling into your trap

But not this time

I'm running away

Never to return

Forgetting about a life

That once existed

Leaving only memories of you

So thanks for letting your truth set you free

I pray your soul feels a little lighter

And the damage I've caused along the years

Will soon dissipate

And I will no longer be a thought

Just remember that I will always love you

But I have to love you from a distance

And I'm okay with that

So no hard feelings

You we're letting your truth set you free

And I thank you

For letting me know

How you truly felt about me

Now when we walk away

It will be a two way street

Not just me looking back

Wondering where you're at

If you're thinking about me

Now I know for sure

That you ain't

And I can go on with my life

I'm breaking the curse

You thought you had upon me

I am about to live my best life

With my name in lights

The ones you said

I couldn't have

That's why I saved this piece

Until the very last

Because I knew you would be trying to find out

What I had to say about you

When you never understood

This was never about you

All I've ever wanted

Was to make you proud

But you were too focused on

Letting your truth set you free

That you could never see the best thing God gave
to you

And we are all equal

I don't have to spell it out

When you understand what I mean

So maybe no one will ever see this book

And that's okay

At least I too

Let my truth set me free

Please...

Be blessed

As I walk out the door

Never to return

Letting our truth set us free

Speakin' The Gospel Truth

Hello...so you reached the end

I hope you've enjoyed

Speakin' The Gospel Truth

I know some things may have rubbed you the
wrong way

But I don't apologize

How I feel inside

It's something that had to come out

Something that God needed to come out

But of course

I don't have to explain it to you

When the truth will set you free

It's all about what you believe

You can look at the glass empty

Or imagine it's half full

Life is all about perception

Standing up for what we believe

Every piece I wrote in this book

Holds near and dear

To my heart

It's the journey that I've grown through

Releasing what's left in my heart

Holding back my greatness

Making me better within

I just found a way

To release

All the things I've been feeling

So in this next life

There will be no chains

Holding me back

From all of my greatness

I will continue Speakin' the Gospel Truth

No matter, how it may make me look

Or come out

I'm on a mission for the Lord

My Savior...Jesus Christ

The one who has many names

You can call him what you like

Those old fears and cares

Have sailed away

They are long gone

When God's word

Is the one I stand on

I can live life abundantly

I guess I just had to find my purpose

Standing on the enemies neck

Breaking him down

Letting him know

He can't defeat God's children

We have faith of a mustard seed

And that's all we need

To watch miracles

Fall from above

So I'm on an assignment

Doing what I've been called to do

Speakin' the Gospel Truth

Telling the world who saved me

Who set me free

And if you don't like it

Well...change the channel

Oh...

This is the end of the book

I have completed God's mission

His basic assignment

Speakin' nothing but God's Gospel Truth

You can love it or leave it

I'm going to drop the mic right here

Because I'm just somebody

Trying to tell everybody

How good God is to me

Speakin' nothing but The Gospel Truth

Thanks for reading my book

About the Author

Tivona Elliott a.k.a. Lady V knew that writing was her passion and escape from the realities of a life of abuse, molestation, and the fast life. Diagnosed with Lupus in 2010, Lady V knew it was time to tell her story; not to hurt the guilty, but to heal from the pain she was enduring within herself. Refusing to allow life to defeat her, she started Fast Life On the Move Radio, Elliott Night Professionals, and added motivational speaker and Life Coach to her resume. Growing from the Pain of Fast Life On the Move, Lady V decided it was time for a change and to embrace her spiritual journey. So she created 2 Gone 2 Long Judgment Free Network. Her goal is to empower, enrich, and encourage others to do great things by teaching people how to keep God first and release, rebuild, and rebrand their lives. No matter what life may throw at her, she will continue to do God's work until God says he's ready for her.

Cash App - $LadyVENP

Linktr.ee/LadyVenp